# DISASTERS

# 1993
# MISSISSIPPI
# River Floods

**Jen Green**

GARETH**STEVENS**
**GS**
PUBLISHING
A WRC Media Company

Please visit our web site at: **www.garethstevens.com**
**For a free color catalog describing Gareth Stevens Publishing's list**
**of high-quality books and multimedia programs, call 1-800-542-2595 (USA)**
**or 1-800-387-3178 (Canada). Gareth Stevens Publishing's fax: (414) 332-3567.**

**Library of Congress Cataloging-in-Publication Data**

Green, Jen.
    1993 Mississippi River floods / Jen Green.
       p. cm. — (Disasters)
    Includes bibliographical references and index.
    ISBN 0-8368-4495-5 (lib. bdg.)
      1. Floods—Mississippi River—Juvenile literature. I. Title: Nineteen ninety
three Mississippi River floods. II. Title. III. Disasters (Milwaukee, Wis.)
    GB1399.4.M7G74   2005
    363.34'93'0977—dc22           2004056704

21439

This edition first published in 2005 by
**Gareth Stevens Publishing**
A WRC Media Company
330 West Olive Street, Suite 100
Milwaukee, Wisconsin 53212 USA

Original copyright © 2004 The Brown Reference Group plc. This U.S. edition
copyright © 2005 by Gareth Stevens, Inc.

Project Editor: Tim Cooke
Consultant: James A. Norwine, Professor of Geography, Texas A&M University
Designer: Lynne Ross
Picture Researcher: Becky Cox

Gareth Stevens series editor: Jenette Donovan Guntly
Gareth Stevens art direction: Tammy West

Picture credits: Front Cover: Corbis: Ed Bock cover
Corbis: 10, 16, 23, Nathan Benn 29, Bettmann 12, Ed Bock title page, 11, Robert Holmes
27, Brooks Kraft 13, Reuters 17, 28, St. Louis Post/Corbis Sygma 5, Jim Shaffer/Corbis
Sygma 18, Ben Spencer/Eye Ubiquitous 15, Les Stone 7, 22, Alison Wright 20; NASA: 14;
Science Photo Library: Pascal Goetgheluck 19; Still Pictures: 8, Fritz Hoffman 25, 26;
USACE: 24, Carol Arney 9.

Maps and Artwork: Brown Reference Group plc

Printed in the United States of America

1 2 3 4 5 6 7 8 9 09 08 07 06 05

**ABOUT THE AUTHOR**
Jen Green holds a doctorate in English and American studies. She has
been a children's author for over 20 years and has written more than
100 books for younger readers on many subjects, including history,
geography, and natural history. She lives in the south of England.

# CONTENTS

**1** THE RISING WATERS  4

**2** THE CAUSES OF RIVER FLOODS  14

**3** AFTERMATH OF THE FLOODS  22

GLOSSARY  30

FURTHER RESEARCH  31

INDEX  32

# 1 THE RISING WATERS

**The "Great Flood" of 1993 was one of the worst disasters in U.S. history. The Mississippi River, Missouri River, and other rivers burst their banks and flooded large areas in nine Midwestern states. The floods damaged property and crops. About seventy thousand people were left homeless.**

An unusually wet fall in 1992 was followed by heavy snowfall through the winter. In March 1993, heavy spring rains and melting snow led to flooding in some areas. As the wet weather continued through April and May, rivers rose higher and higher.

Above the Midwest, cool, dry air from Canada hit damp, warm air coming up from the Gulf of Mexico. As the warm air cooled, it shed its **moisture** in a series of rain showers. By early June 1993, about three times as much rain had fallen in parts of the Midwest in just eight months than usually fell in a whole year.

► The waters of the Mississippi flooded the countryside south of St. Louis, Missouri, on August 1, 1993. Crops were damaged and farm animals were killed by the floods.

### THE FLOODS BEGIN

The first rivers flooded in Minnesota and Wisconsin. As they drained into larger rivers, the flooding moved downstream toward the Mississippi River. The Corps of **Engineers**, the

# MIGHTY MISSISSIPPI

The Mississippi is North America's largest river. It flows for about 2,340 miles (3,770 kilometers) from Lake Itasca in Minnesota to the Gulf of Mexico. The river and its **tributaries** drain the vast basin between the Rocky Mountains and the Appalachian Mountains. The river system is important as a route for ships.

The Mississippi River can be divided into two parts. The Upper Mississippi runs from Lake Itasca to Thebes, Illinois, where it is joined by the Ohio River. The Lower Mississippi runs from Thebes to the Gulf of Mexico. The 1993 floods only affected the upper section of the river.

▲ **The Mississippi and its tributaries drain the land in the heart of the United States. The blue area covering the land shows where the floods happened.**

## FACT FILE

**WHERE:**

Mississippi River Valley, Midwestern United States

**WHEN:**

June–August 1993

**TOTAL TIME:**

Three months

**TOTAL AREA:**

Flooded 31,000 square miles (80,000 square kilometers) of nine states

**COSTS:**

$20 billion damage to property, plus losses to businesses

**KILLED OR INJURED:**

48 dead

U.S. Army's group of building experts, decided to act. The corps takes care of levees, which are raised banks made of dirt or crushed stone and which stop rivers from overflowing. The engineers closed lock gates, which control the river's water level. Ships could no longer pass along the river. Ships on the Mississippi carry about 175 million tons (159 million tonnes) of cargo each year from St. Paul, Minnesota, to the coast near Baton Rouge, Louisiana. Stopping the ships cost $1 million a day.

### FACING THE RISING WATERS

By early July 1993, more than one hundred rivers in the Mississippi River Basin had flooded. Along the Upper Mississippi River,

▼ A chain of volunteers piles sandbags in the city of St. Louis, Missouri. The sand in the bags soaks up water and prevents more water from passing through the bags and flooding lands surrounding the river.

► **Water spreads on both sides of this broken levee, or raised bank, near Quincy, Illinois. A construction crew is trying to repair the hole in the levee.**

## EYEWITNESS

*"We went from the river where we had the river boats break loose. Part of the flood wall was failing. The river was going to an unprecedented record high of forty-nine feet [14.94 meters], for sure, we knew then. . . . The Corps of Engineers was telling us, 'We're not sure how much higher the river is going to go.' All of our levees and our makeshift sandbag levees were failing all at one time. And then, all of a sudden, it was just like God decided we had enough."*

NEIL SVETANICS,
ST. LOUIS, MISSOURI

the Missouri River, and smaller rivers, people and soldiers from the **National Guard** stacked millions of sandbags to strengthen the levees. When levees failed, people put sandbags in the doors and windows of their homes and businesses to stop the water from coming in.

The Corps of Engineers set up emergency centers. It moved people out of their homes and rescued stranded people. The corps also gave out food, clean water, and medicine. People whose homes were flooded stayed in tents and other shelters.

The flooding caused many health worries. Drains overflowed and sewage flowed into

# FLOOD DEFENSES

Building guards to protect towns and cities from floods along the Mississippi River began in the early eighteenth century. People built levees along the banks of the river. Throughout the nineteenth century, people continued to build banks and other guards against floods. Some people did not believe the defenses would help. Writer Mark Twain (1835–1910) wrote: "You cannot tame that lawless stream. . . . The Mississippi will always have its own way; no engineering skill can persuade it to do otherwise."

In the 1930s, following terrible floods in 1927 (see box on page 12), the U.S. Army Corps of Engineers built many dams, **reservoirs**, and levees to contain floods along the Mississippi River and the smaller rivers that run into it. Most dams and reservoirs protecting the Mississippi are located on the Upper Missouri River, where they do not get in the way of shipping. By the 1990s, there were flood defenses along about 2,000 miles (3,200 km) of riverbank.

▼ **This lock and dam near Rock Island, Illinois, are part of the Mississippi's flood defenses. By opening or closing dams, engineers can control the flow of water in the river.**

# BUILDING IN THE MISSISSIPPI RIVER BASIN

Building guards against floods on the Mississippi River in the twentieth century allowed a lot of land along the river to be used for farming, industry, and housing. Between 1940 and 1990, about four-fifths of the **wetlands** along the region's rivers were drained, which created new land for farms, factories, and houses. Farmers, factory owners, and home buyers were eager to buy land along the river banks, where real estate was cheap and the soil was good for growing crops. The land along the river had acted as a sponge, however. It soaked up floodwater when the rivers rose. Without it, more water ran off the land back into the rivers. More water in the rivers increased the chance of flooding.

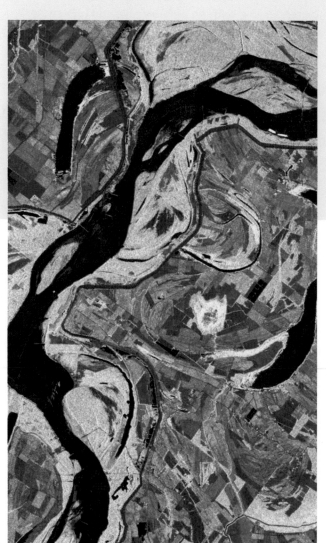

▼ The light-green parts of this colorized satellite image show the Mississippi River's floodplains, which are flat pieces of land that often flood.

streets and homes, which made water supplies dirty. Des Moines, Iowa, had no drinking water for nearly three weeks. It was the longest a U.S. city had ever gone without safe water.

In the countryside, floods covered thousands of square miles (sq km) of crops. Farmers battled to get terrified farm animals onto rafts and boats.

▶ **People stuck in remote places like this flooded farm in the Midwest were rescued by helicopter.**

## EYEWITNESS

"It's like getting kicked in the gut. And you know, it was probably the worst day of my life. . . . Even in our faintest imagination, we never thought the levees were going to fail. We always thought we were going to beat it. You know how you always figure hard work and determination will take care of everything. Well, it's not necessarily so. You can't beat Mother Nature sometimes. It was a real cruel lesson to learn. Like I said, it probably was the worst day of my life."

*DAVE MUELLER, U.S. ARMY CORPS OF ENGINEERS*

### THE RAINS CONTINUE

Heavy rain kept falling. From June through August 1993, more than 2 feet (0.6 meters) of rain fell in Kansas and Missouri. In Iowa, the state's eastern and western borders are formed by the Missouri and Mississippi Rivers. During that time, the region received a record 4 feet (1.2 m) of rain. The swollen floodwaters moved down the rivers. By mid-July, parts of nine Midwestern states were under water and rivers were at record high levels.

Communities hit by the floods included St. Paul and Minneapolis in Minnesota, and south from Rock Island to Cairo, Illinois. On

11

the Missouri River, the flood area stretched from Nebraska City, Nebraska, through Kansas to St. Charles in Missouri. President Bill Clinton declared much of the Upper Mississippi River Basin a disaster area.

## FLOODING ON THE MISSISSIPPI RIVER

Floods are common events along the Mississippi River, mainly in spring when snow melts and adds to water brought by heavy spring rains. The 1993 floods were the worst since damaging floods in 1927. The 1927 floods had covered nearly 27,000 square miles (69,000 sq km) of land along the Lower Mississippi River and made about 700,000 people homeless. The 1927 flood drowned 246 people, along with 165,000 farm animals. It caused damage totaling $364 million. Ten years later, in 1937, floods created a lake in the Lower Mississippi River Basin almost the size of Lake Superior, one of the Great Lakes. It later drained away. Floods struck again in the 1940s and 1950s, with more severe flooding in 1965 and 1973.

▲ A man rows a boat down a flooded street after the Mississippi River flood of 1927.

In early August, St. Louis, Missouri, held its breath. The city lies in a bend between the Mississippi and Missouri Rivers. Floodwaters raged toward the city. If it flooded, millions of people would be affected. The river level rose to 49 feet (15 m), just 3 feet (1 m) below the top of the high wall that protected St. Louis.

About August 10, the rains stopped at last and river levels began to drop. The floodwaters spilled back into the rivers through broken levees. The floods had left forty-eight people dead, and many thousands of people homeless. It had damaged or destroyed crops, homes, and businesses and killed farm animals. Now the cleanup could begin.

▼ **Residents look at a flooded street in Des Moines, Iowa. The floods shut down the city's water system for three weeks. The disaster cost businesses millions of dollars.**

13

# 2 THE CAUSES OF RIVER FLOODS

**Floods are the most common of all natural disasters, and they do the most damage. More people die in floods each year than in all other kinds of natural disasters put together, including hurricanes and earthquakes.**

Floods happen when a river fills with more water than it can hold. The extra water overflows the banks and runs into the low-lying lands around the river.

Throughout history, people have settled by rivers. Rivers provide good soil for farming, fish for food, and a way to travel and move goods. People in early societies farmed by rivers in China, India, and Egypt. As well as helping people, however, rivers bring the risk of floods, which can drown people and animals and damage property.

◄ From space, the Nile Valley is a green strip in the desert of Egypt. The Nile River floods regularly. The floodwaters carry rich soil onto the land. When the floodwaters flow back into the river, the rich soil is left behind. Ancient Egyptians settled along the Nile River because it was a good place to grow food. The river was also an important means of moving people and goods from place to place.

## RAINS AND FLOODS

The most common cause of river flooding is heavy rainfall. The water drains into rivers and streams. In spring, rainwater can combine with melting snow to increase the chance of flooding. Parts of the world, such as southern Asia, are often hit by floods during the annual rainy season. Monsoons are winds that change direction each season. In some seasons, they are dry winds that blow from the land out to sea. In other seasons, when they blow in off the ocean, they carry clouds full of moisture, which cause heavy rain.

Other causes of river floods include broken dams, rough seas, and high tides, which can push water up rivers to cause flooding. Some floods can last weeks or months. Flash floods, on the other hand, are short, but they can be

▼ Seasonal rains pour down on the city of Simla in India. The regular rainy season brings heavy rain almost daily. The rain can cause serious river flooding.

# FLASH FLOOD ON THE BIG THOMPSON RIVER

In July 1976, the Big Thompson River Valley in Colorado's Rocky Mountains was struck by one of the worst flash floods in U.S. history. The flood was caused by a heavy downpour that dumped about 12 inches (30 centimeters) of rain in less than five hours. As the waters raged through the narrow Big Thompson Canyon, it swept away roads, houses, cars, and bridges. The flood killed 139 people, and repairing the damage cost $35 million.

▶ **The Big Thompson River flood washed out Highway 34 and left a trail of damage in Colorado.**

very violent. Flash floods happen when heavy rain falls on steep land and runs off the land very quickly. Flash floods also happen where rivers are too narrow to hold extra water. In most cases, the floods last less than an hour.

Some scientists believe that humans are increasing the risk of flooding. For example, when people cut down forests, more rainwater runs into rivers. This is because trees act as sponges and soak up rain. When people drain water from the land along rivers in order to build on it, it also reduces the land's ability to soak up water, as does building new structures that cover the ground with concrete.

▼ **These homes in China were flooded in 2002. Since ancient times, people have risked living in China's river valleys, which are often flooded. Floods on the Yangtze River have caused so much damage that the river is sometimes called "China's Sorrow."**

### RIVER SCIENCE

The study of Earth's water supplies is called hydrology. Hydrologists study how much water a river can hold. They also set up measuring stations on rivers with tools for checking how

# WHAT CAUSED THE MISSISSIPPI RIVER FLOOD OF 1993?

Experts studying the Great Flood say there were four main causes of the disaster. Long and heavy rainfall during the first six months of 1993 was the main problem. Another problem was individual rain storms that shed such huge amounts of water that streams and rivers could not hold the water. In addition, scientists say that the ground was still soaked from the rains of 1992. The temperatures were cooler than usual, and so water from the 1992 rains had not been **evaporated** by the Sun's heat.  The fourth cause was man-made. Many of the experts say that building structures along the Mississippi River, including building levees, made matters worse.

▼ **Experts believe that building structures, such as this highway interchange, on the Mississippi floodplain makes the land less able to absorb water, which increases the risk of floods.**

fast the rivers are flowing. The stations help scientists study how much water is in rivers and how fast the water is flowing.

Hydrologists who work for the United States **Geological** Survey (USGS) check rivers that are at risk of flooding. The scientists put weather data into computers to see when rivers like the Mississippi River might flood. This allows them to give flood warnings. USGS experts also give advice to engineers about where they should build bridges, roads, or buildings along rivers.

### WHAT CAN BE DONE ABOUT FLOODS?

Scientists cannot stop the weather conditions that cause floods. There are, however, actions that may limit the damage floods cause. The actions include building guards, such as dams, or other barriers called weirs, which often

▶ **A hydrologist stains a river with a special dye. By timing how long it takes the dye to flow down to different parts of the river, it is possible to measure the river's flow rate, which is how quickly the water is moving.**

▲ Cutting down trees in forests, like what is shown here on the Javari River in Peru, adds to the **runoff into rivers**. The runoff increases because trees help soak up rainwater. Their roots also hold soil in place and prevent the soil from being washed into river channels.

have gates that can increase or decrease the amount of water flowing through. Floodways provide places where extra water can flow out of the river. Types of floodways include reservoirs, swamps, and canals, which are man-made rivers. In addition to helping to prevent floods, the flow of water through dams may also be used to produce electricity, while floodways help water the land for farming.

Other forms of guards against flooding include building levees, which help keep water in river channels, and making new wetlands, which can soak up extra water.

Good farming practices, including not draining land along rivers, and careful planning of new building projects can cut the risk of floods as well. Planners know which places are at greatest risk of flooding so that new homes and other structures can be built elsewhere. Some buildings that are already in place can be flood-proofed, which means that the buildings are protected by being raised on stilts or by being surrounded with steel or concrete walls. Flood-warning systems also give people time to move out of the way when danger threatens. Systems are already being used in many high-risk regions in the United States.

# THE WATER CYCLE

Water is key to all living things, but almost all water on Earth is salty. The planet's tiny amount of **freshwater** is found in rivers, streams, lakes, and the **polar ice caps**. It is also found underground. Water moves between the air, oceans, and dry land in a loop called the hydrological, or water, cycle. The Sun's warmth causes moisture to evaporate from seas, lakes, and sheets of ice in the form of **water vapor** (1). High in the air, water droplets **condense** and collect to form clouds, which later shed rain, snow, or hail (2). The rain or snow that falls on land and that is not soaked up by the soil or plants or used by people drains back into streams and rivers (3). The streams and rivers run back into lakes or oceans, to complete the loop.

▼ **This diagram shows the cycle by which water moves around the planet.**

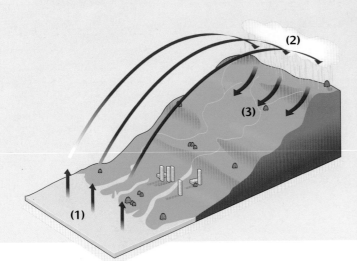

# 3 AFTERMATH OF THE FLOODS

In early September 1993, the floodwaters of the Mississippi River finally dropped enough to allow people to clean up the damage. A month of flooding had left a huge mess. Thick gray mud coated everything.

Tons of wreckage, such as rotten plaster, wet carpets, and even catfish carried in by the floods, had to be cleared from buildings up and down the region's rivers. Brown, rotting crops filled the fields in the countryside, while trees and shrubs were stripped of leaves.

▼ In all, about seventy thousand people were forced out of their homes by the floods. This family in Quincy, Illinois, was among the homeless.

People from the Midwest began the task of cleaning up the mess, helped by volunteers and the National Guard. Groups such as the Red Cross, Salvation Army, and churches provided medicine and hot meals. They helped comfort people who had lost their homes. Officials from the Federal Emergency Management Agency (FEMA) gave out funds to help people pay for the cleanup. Congress voted to give a total of $5.7 billion to help. Some people had also bought insurance, which paid them money when their homes were flooded.

▲ Army engineers provide safe drinking water in Des Moines, Iowa. The floods filled all the drains and mixed dirty water with the town's drinking water. Providing safe water to drink was very important since drinking dirty water can spread diseases.

### IMPACT OF THE FLOODS

The area of the damage was huge. At its height, the Great Flood covered 31,000 square miles (80,000 sq km) of land. More than fifty-six thousand homes were wrecked or damaged. Roads, bridges, and railroads were damaged, along with gas lines, power lines, water

# DO LEVEES WORK?

After the 1993 floods, the Army Corps of Engineers studied how the Mississippi River's flood defenses had worked. A total of 5,760 miles (9,270 km) of levees were damaged. They were mainly levees owned by residents, but nearly one-fifth of government-owned levees were also broken. Experts said that most of the levees that failed had been built to keep out water only for a few days. Instead, the 1993 floods lasted for weeks. Some scientists believe that levees actually increased the damage because the levees attempted to keep the rising water in the rivers, rather than allowing it to run off onto surrounding land. Other scientists say that the levees kept the damage from being even worse.

▼ **This photograph shows barges, used to ship goods on the Mississippi River, beside a levee near New Orleans, Louisiana, in 1999. Some experts still believe that levees are the best defense against floods.**

24

supplies, and sewage systems, which were important for keeping people healthy. The bill to repair the damage was almost $20 billion.

The Great Flood hurt the economy of the Midwest. The Mississippi River was closed to ships for more than two months, which stopped the shipping of millions of tons (tonnes) of grain, oil, and other products. Thousands of acres (hectares) of soybeans, corn, and wheat crops were ruined. Businesses also had to replace ruined goods and repair flooded buildings. In Des Moines, Iowa, for example, businesses lost about $716 million.

On the positive side, the city of St. Louis, Missouri, mostly escaped the floods. Also,

▼ **The floodwaters wrecked many homes throughout the Midwest. Some homes were so weakened that they had to be pulled down. Those that survived were full of sand and mud. Many of the contents of the buildings were ruined.**

**▲ A bulldozer plows through the mud left on riverside fields by the floods. In places, the silt, or river mud left by the floodwaters, was up to 10 feet (3 m) deep.**

only forty-eight people died in the disaster. Flood warnings that allowed people to escape the floods and the work of groups such as the Corps of Engineers stopped more people from dying. Although 150 rivers in the Upper Mississippi River Basin burst their banks, the Lower Mississippi was mainly free of flooding. Most of the Ohio River, which feeds into the Mississippi, also did not flood. Along these stretches of river, the water stayed in wider, deeper channels or ran into reservoirs.

### RECOVERY AND LESSONS LEARNED

In the months after the Great Flood, many broken levees were rebuilt. Other parts of the land along the river have been left as wetlands, which many scientists believe will help cut the risk of future floods. The wetlands will soak up water during heavy rains. Some parts of the floodplain have been replanted with trees. Elsewhere, hillsides have been shaped and new floodways built to cut runoff into the rivers. There are also new rules about building on the floodplain. Officials have limited new construction in some of the worst-hit regions.

About twenty-six thousand people left their homes during the Great Flood. Some never returned to live there. Most people, however, came back within a few months.

Many of the people forced to leave their homes during the flood did not have much money. Many small-farm owners, businesses, and young families had moved onto the

▼ **A ship transports cargo on the Lower Mississippi near New Orleans, Louisiana. Shipping on the river was shut down for more than two months. The loss of business cost millions of dollars.**

## GLOBAL WARMING

Scientists say that the risk of flooding will increase because temperatures are going up around the world. This problem, called global warming, is leading to higher sea levels because ice in cold regions is melting. More water is now evaporating into the atmosphere, so wet parts of the world are becoming wetter. Global warming may be caused by burning fuels, such as oil and coal. The fuels release gases into the air, which trap heat near Earth and raise temperatures.

▼ National Guardsmen check the Mississippi River from a levee made of sandbags in Davenport, Iowa, in April 2001. The people of the town had decided not to build a permanent wall to defend the town against floods.

low-lying river land because real estate there was cheap. Few people had insurance to pay for flood damage. Instead, they hoped to get money from FEMA and other groups.

Since the disaster, more people who live in areas near the Mississippi River have bought flood insurance, but many people still feel it costs too much. Meanwhile, towns near the river, such as Davenport, Iowa, are blamed for not building guards against floods. In order to keep the town's view of the river, the people of Davenport did not build a flood wall. Instead, the townspeople had planned to ask for money from FEMA to pay for cleanup after floods.

Experts think that a disaster as severe as the Great Flood will only happen once in a century. Still, as one victim of that flood said, "It's going to be a long time before people around here don't panic every time it starts to rain."

▲ **The Ohio River and the Mississippi River meet north of St. Louis, Missouri. Whatever people in that area do to avoid disaster, each year, spring rains bring the risk of flooding along the mighty rivers of the Midwest.**

# GLOSSARY

**condense** Change from a gas to a liquid or solid. When water in warm, damp air cools, it collects to become droplets, such as rain.

**engineers** People who are trained to work with engines or to make or build things.

**evaporated** Turned from a liquid into a vapor or gas when heated.

**freshwater** Related to being of or living in water that is not salty.

**geological** Related to geology; geology is the study of soil, rocks, and minerals and what they tell us about the history of Earth.

**lock** A section of a river that has gates at each end, allowing water to be pumped in or out to raise or lower that section's water level.

**moisture** Small amounts of liquid, such as water, that are present in the air or in the ground and that make objects or the air feel damp.

**National Guard** A branch of the U.S. military that is only active when called upon by a state or by the federal government.

**polar ice caps** The large sheets of ice or snow that cover large areas of land at the North and South Poles all year round.

**reservoir** A man-made lake in which a large amount of water is collected and stored for later use.

**runoff** Rain or melted snow that flows from the land into rivers and streams.

**tributaries** Rivers or streams that flow into larger rivers or streams.

**water vapor** Water in the form of a gas. It is created when water is heated. It collects to form clouds.

**wetlands** Areas of land where the soil is always wet, including near waterways that often overflow.

# FURTHER RESEARCH

## BOOKS

Badt, Karin Luisa. *The Mississippi Flood of 1993* (Cornerstones of Freedom, Second series). Children's Press, 1994.

Bredeson, Carmen. *The Mighty Midwest Flood: Raging Rivers.* (American Disasters) Enslow Publishers, 1999.

Green, Jen. *The Mississippi River (Rivers of North America).* Gareth Stevens, 2004.

Hiscock, Bruce. *The Big Rivers: The Missouri, the Mississippi, and the Ohio.* Atheneum, 1997.

Lauber, Patricia. *Flood.* National Geographic, 1996.

Meister, Cari. *Floods (Nature's Fury).* Abdo and Daughters Publishing, 2000.

Vogel, Carole G. *The Great Midwest Flood.* Little Brown and Co, 1995.

## WEB SITES

*Flood!*
www.pbs.org/wgbh/nova/flood

*The Great Flood of 1993, United States Geological Service (USGS)*
mo.water.usgs.gov/Reports/1993-Flood/Index.htm

*IN FOCUS: FLOODS*
www.pbs.org/newshour/infocus/floods.htm/

*Looking Back, American Red Cross*
www.redcross.org/news/ds/floods/030806midwest93.html

*Mississippi Flood of 1993, David McConnell, University of Akron*
lists.uakron.edu/geology/natscigeo/lectures/streams/miss_flood.htm

# INDEX

Big Thompson River 16

businesses 13, 25

Cairo, Illinois 11

cargo 7, 27

causes of floods 14, 15, 16, 17, 18

China 14, 17

Clinton, Bill 12

Corps of Engineers 4, 7, 8, 9, 24, 26

crops 10, 22, 25

damage 13, 25

Davenport, Iowa 28, 29

Des Moines, Missouri 10, 13, 23, 25

Egypt 14

farmers 10, 25, 27

Federal Emergency Management Agency (FEMA) 23, 28, 29

flash floods 15, 16

flood of 1927 12

flood of 1937 12

flood warnings 19, 21

global warming 28

health dangers 8, 10

homeless people 13, 22

hydrologists 17, 19

Iowa 11

India 14

insurance 28

Kansas 11, 12

levees 7, 8, 9, 18, 20, 24, 26, 28

lock gates 7, 9

Minnesota 4, 11

Mississippi River 4, 6, 7, 9, 10, 11, 13, 18, 19, 22, 24, 25, 26, 28, 29

Missouri River 4, 8, 11, 12, 13

monsoons 15

National Guard 8, 23, 28

Nebraska City, Nebraska 12

New Orleans 24, 27

Nile River 14

Ohio River 26, 29

Quincy, Illinois 8, 22

rainfall 4, 11, 15, 18

Rock Island, Illinois 9, 11

sandbags 7, 8, 28

St. Charles, Missouri 12

St. Louis, Missouri 4, 7, 13, 25

St. Paul, Minnesota 11

ships 7, 25, 27

Twain, Mark 9

United States Geological Survey (USGS) 19

water cycle 21

water supplies 10, 23

weirs 19

wetlands 26, 27

Wisconsin 4

Yangtze River 17